religion in focus
hinduism

Geoff Teece

First published in 2003 by Franklin Watts
Franklin Watts, 96 Leonard Street, London EC2A 4XD

Franklin Watts Australia
45–51 Huntley Street, Alexandria, NSW 2015
This edition published under license from Franklin Watts. All rights reserved.

Copyright © 2003 Franklin Watts

Series Editor: Adrian Cole; Designer: Proof Books; Art Director: Jonathan Hair; Consultant: Rasamandala Das, co-director of ISKCON Educational Services; Picture Researcher: Diana Morris

Published in the United States by Smart Apple Media
1980 Lookout Drive, North Mankato, Minnesota 56003

U.S. publication copyright © 2005 Smart Apple Media
International copyright reserved in all countries. No part of this book may be reproduced in any form without written permission from the publisher.

Library of Congress Cataloging-in-Publication Data

Teece, Geoff.
Hinduism / Geoff Teece.
p. cm. — (Religion in focus)
Includes index.
Contents: Origins and history—God and the gods—Shakti and Avatars—Key concepts and the journey of life—Family and life rituals—Scriptures—Worship and the Mandir—Sacred places—Festivals—Values.
ISBN 1-58340-466-X
1. Hinduism—Juvenile literature. [1. Hinduism.] I. Title. II. Series.

BL1203.T44 2005
294.5—dc22   2003061730

9 8 7 6 5 4 3 2 1

Contents

ORIGINS AND HISTORY 4

GOD AND THE GODS 6

SHAKTI AND AVATARS 8

KEY CONCEPTS AND THE JOURNEY OF LIFE 10

FAMILY AND LIFE RITUALS 14

SCRIPTURES 16

WORSHIP AND THE MANDIR 18

SACRED PLACES 22

FESTIVALS 24

VALUES 28

KEY QUESTIONS AND ANSWERS 30

GLOSSARY 31

INDEX 32

God and the gods

Many Hindus believe there is one God who is worshiped in different forms, an idea that stems from the very earliest Hindu scriptures. This one supreme being is named Brahman, though Hindus often address God in more personal ways, using such words as *Bhagavan*, or the name of a particular deity, such as Vishnu.

BRAHMAN

Brahman is the eternal truth that creates and supports the universe—like space, it is present in everything and yet beyond it. Brahman (eternal spirit) is different from physical matter (*prakriti*), which is always changing. This is first understood by recognizing that the *atman* (individual soul) is different from the temporary material body.

Hindus use the sacred symbol "Om" to stand for Brahman. It can be found in many temples. Om is the original sound by which the Supreme created the universe. Hindus often chant "Om" when they meditate or worship.

THE TRIMURTI

The life force of Brahman is represented by the *Trimurti* (three-form), which is made up of three main deities. These are Brahma (the creator of the universe), Vishnu (the preserver of the universe), and Shiva (the destroyer—although some Hindus believe he also has a role in re-creation).

The word *murti* means "form" and refers to the sacred images of God. Sometimes the word "deity" is used instead of *murti*. The three *murtis*, or deities, are not entirely separate, but are different aspects and forms of God in relation to this world.

BRAHMA (the creator)

The *murti* of Brahma is usually pictured with four faces, each one pointing towards one of the four points of the compass. This symbolizes that God created the whole universe. Brahma is worshiped only in Pushkar, India.

VISHNU (the preserver)

Vishnu preserves the harmony and order of the universe. To help maintain this natural order, worshipers need to understand right and wrong, and live good spiritual lives according to their *dharma*. The symbols connected with Vishnu remind them of their responsibilities. Vishnu is usually shown either lying on a snake or with a snake behind his head. This symbolizes cosmic time and energy. The color blue represents his endless spiritual power. He has four hands that often hold a conch shell (symbolizing the music of the universe, calling people to live a pure life), a discus or chakra (representing time and the punishment of wrongdoers), a mace (representing his royal authority and ability to protect the world from evil), and a lotus flower (symbolizing purity and spiritual enlightenment).

VISHNU

There are many symbols associated with Vishnu that remind worshipers of their responsibilities.

SHIVA (the destroyer and re-creator of the universe)

Shiva is seen in three different forms. In the form of Shiva Nataraj, or "lord of the dance," he is shown dancing the world into existence within a circle of fire. He stands on a demon representing *avidya* (ignorance of spiritual truth). The tension between *avidya* and wisdom (knowledge) is central to the Hindu tradition. Hindus believe everyone must turn away from *avidya* in order to re-identify with Brahman, the Supreme, and achieve *moksha*.

In another form, Shiva is shown as a man meditating (a *yogi*) with the Himalayas in the background. This shows that he has pure concentration and is not distracted by earthly things. A cobra around his neck symbolizes that he is beyond death, and a tiger skin over his shoulder represents the need to overcome ignorance and pride. His trident is the symbol of a holy man who has given up the pleasures of an earthly life.

The third aspect of Shiva is the *lingum*. This symbolizes Shiva's creative and reviving powers. It is a rounded stone pillar (representing the male reproductive organ or *linga*) set in a circular stone (representing the *yoni*, the female reproductive organ). This form of Shiva is worshiped only in temples.

SHIVA NATARAJ

Shiva, in the form of Shiva Nataraj, dances within a circle, which represents the eternal cycle of time.

7

Shakti and avatars

DURGA
Durga is a strong warrior goddess. In each of her eight hands she has different weapons with which to kill Mahishasura, the buffalo demon.

In addition to worshipers of Vishnu and Shiva (Brahma is rarely worshiped), there is also a third, large group of Hindus that worship Shakti.

SHAKTI

Shakti represents Mother Nature. Shakti specifically refers to the consort of Shiva, but worship of Shakti may include other goddesses, such as Lakshmi and Saraswati (the wives of Vishnu and Brahma respectively).

On her own, the goddess takes the form of two powerful figures called Durga and Kali. Durga rides a lion or tiger, illustrating her great strength and control, and carries weapons to kill the buffalo demon of ignorance. In the form of Kali, the goddess is at her most terrifying. She is shown black or dark in color with many heads and a tongue dripping with blood. She wears a garland of skulls and holds a severed head in her hand. These symbols represent her great power in destroying evil.

As the consort of Shiva, the goddess is called Parvati or Uma and represents the gentle side of her nature as a loving wife. The consort of Vishnu is called Lakshmi, the goddess of wealth and good fortune. The consort of Brahma is called Saraswati, the goddess of learning and the arts. She holds the sacred scriptures and plays a *vina* (an Indian musical instrument, like a sitar).

VAISHNAVAS AND SHAIVAS

Not all Hindus believe that the various deities are equal, representing different aspects of an impersonal God. Instead, they consider one or more deities to be supreme, giving the others a lower position. There are two main groups: most Vaishnavas believe Vishnu is God himself, while many Shaivas consider Shiva to be the Supreme. Devotion to Vishnu is the more popular belief.

Vishnu can take many forms, especially the form of an *avatar*, which means "one who descends." There are 10 *avatars* of Vishnu, and the most important of these are Krishna and Rama.

KRISHNA

Krishna is said to have lived on earth about 5,000 years ago. He is usually pictured with a flute, which symbolizes the heavenly music that he brings into the world. He is also pictured with a cow—a sacred animal in India that symbolizes the importance of the mother figure. Stories of Krishna's life are told in the *Mahabharata* (*see pages 16–17*), including how he taught about the different spiritual paths (*yogas*) and the importance of being unselfish. In 1966, the International Society for Krishna Consciousness (ISKCON) was founded. This is a movement devoted to worshiping Krishna as the Supreme.

KRISHNA
Krishna is an *avatar* of Vishnu. His birth is celebrated during Janmashtami (*see pages 26–27*).

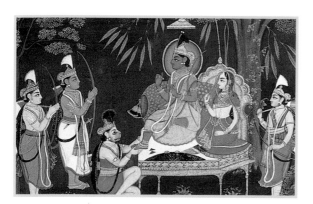

RAMA

Rama symbolizes great courage and is the ideal man. His *murti* shows him with a bow and arrows. The *Ramayana* (*see page 17*) tells his story, which illustrates how good always overcomes evil.

RAMA
Rama is an *avatar* of Vishnu. He represents virtue and courage.

THE 10 AVATARS OF VISHNU (*shown right*)

1. Matsya, the fish who helped save the *Vedas*.

2. Kurma, the turtle who assisted the gods and demons in churning the ocean of milk.

3. Varaha, the boar who fought a terrible demon.

4. Narasimha, the half-man, half-lion who killed a demon that stopped people from worshiping God.

5. Vamana, the dwarf whose toe pierced the wall of the universe, letting in the water that became the river Ganges.

6. Parusha-Rama; he killed many leaders who had become corrupt.

7. Rama, who rescued his wife from a demon (*see above*).

8. Krishna, the cowherd boy (*see above*).

9. Buddha, because he taught the world about enlightenment (not all Hindus regard Buddha as an *avatar*).

10. Kalki, who is due to come at the end of the present time (called the Kali yuga). He will return peace and holiness to the world.

9

Key concepts and the journey of life

THE WHEEL OF LIFE

For Hindus, life is a journey from one body to another, and each life is in itself a journey from birth to death. Along the journey there are "signposts" to follow that enable a person to get closer to God.

SAMSARA, MOKSHA, AND THE EFFECT OF KARMA

The bodies of most Hindus are cremated after death. But while the ashes of the body return to the earth, the individual soul (*atman*) continues its journey through the cycle of reincarnation, called *samsara*. Hindu scriptures say that death is simply like casting off one set of clothes and putting on a new one.

The cycle of reincarnation is not seen as something to be joyful about. *Samsara* is a tiring wheel of suffering and misery. The goal for Hindus is to escape *samsara* and reach *moksha* (spiritual freedom). On the wheel of life the soul must obey the law of cause and effect, called *karma*. The body into which a soul is reborn depends on its *karma*—how that soul acted in its previous life. Good deeds lead to a better standard of life and greater freedom and, if directed towards the divine, bring *moksha*. Selfish and ignorant deeds lead to suffering, such as being born into a lower species, and increased bondage to the cycle of repeated birth and death.

AVIDYA AND MAYA

In order to escape *samsara* and achieve *moksha*, everyone must turn away from *avidya* (ignorance of spiritual truth). *Avidya* results in *maya* (illusion—having the wrong ideas about what really matters and what is really true). For example, *maya* may convince a person that material possessions will bring lasting happiness. Attachment to material things, including the human body, keeps people bound to this world. Earthly attachments can also come from the emotions. Powerful feelings such as lust, greed, and anger make people unaware of their true identity, which is that of Brahman (eternal, full of knowledge and bliss).

Shankara (*see page 4*) taught that the *atman* (individual soul) is like a droplet of water that belongs in the ocean of Brahman. The problem is that because of *avidya* people do not realize this—they prefer to ignore the truth.

DISCARDING EARTHLY ATTACHMENTS (*OPPOSITE PAGE*)

After death, the *atman* (individual soul) continues its tiring journey through the cycle of reincarnation. The *atman* tries to escape this cycle and join Brahman, in the same way that a droplet of water becomes part of the ocean.

AVIDYA: ignorance of spiritual truth.

MAYA: illusion—having the wrong ideas about what really matters and what is really true.

10

THE FOUR ASHRAMAS

A Hindu's spiritual journey follows the natural process of growing up. Life is divided into four stages, called *ashramas*. Each *ashrama* stresses its own *dharma*, rather than a fixed set of beliefs. *Dharma* are the duties that support a person's spiritual (eternal) and human (temporary) nature.

BRAHMACHARYA, OR STUDENT

Brahmacharya, or the student stage, is the first *ashrama* and begins with the initiation of the sacred thread (*see page 14*). Traditionally, only the three highest *varnas* have practiced this *ashrama*. It involves following a *dharma* of gaining religious knowledge, especially of the *Vedas* (ancient scriptures). In the past, students left home between the ages of 8 and 16 and went to a special school to be taught by a guru (teacher). Today, students attend ordinary schools, but it is still considered essential that a young person learns about the scriptures and develops proper attitudes, especially towards teachers and parents.

BRAHMACHARYA
This is the first *ashrama*. It begins with the initiation of the sacred thread.

GRIHASTA, OR HOUSEHOLDER

The second *ashrama* is that of *grihasta*, or householder. This stage is based on two of the Hindu aims in life: *artha* (earning an honest living and providing for the family) and *kama* (enjoying the pleasures of life). A householder's *dharma* is focused on being a good husband or wife and a good parent. Most people cannot achieve *moksha* without first accepting the responsibilities of everyday life.

GRIHASTA
This is the second *ashrama*. It is based on raising a family.

12

VANAPRASTHA, OR RETIREMENT STAGE

The third *ashrama* is *vanaprastha*, or the retirement stage. This is a time when a person's *dharma* switches from the earthly duties of the householder to a more spiritual path focused on at non-attachment, meditation, and study of the scriptures. Traditionally, this stage begins when a person's children are grown up and a son is born to the first son. This ensures the continuation of the family.

SANNYASA, OR WORLD RENOUNCER

The fourth and final stage is called *sannyasa*, or world renouncer. This stage is taken up by very few Hindus, but is seen as an ideal. The *sannyasi* gives up all possessions and becomes a wandering holy man with no fixed home. A *sannyasi* concentrates solely on *moksha*.

A SANNYASI
Many *sannyasis* can be found in India, often wandering from place to place. Their basic needs, such as food, are supplied by local people as a form of charity.

13

Family and life rituals

Family life is very important for Hindus. In India, several generations of one family often live together. They celebrate many special ceremonies called *samskaras*, which are performed throughout a Hindu's life. *Samskaras* are acts of purification, and Hindus believe that they provide direction along the journey of life from birth to death. There are 16 *samskaras* in all, but the largest are held for the birth of a baby, initiation of the sacred thread, marriage, and death.

BIRTH

A newborn baby is welcomed into the world by putting a small amount of honey on its tongue. A prayer is also whispered into the baby's ear: "May God the creator of all things grant you firm wisdom. Knowledge and wisdom are the sources of power and long life."

About 11 days after the birth, a naming ceremony is performed. This is when the mother usually has her first bath since giving birth, the father shaves for the first time since the birth, and the house is filled with fresh flowers. These are all rituals of purification and symbols of new life. The priest casts a horoscope for the child to decide the first letter of his or her name. Hindu children are traditionally given names that have meanings. Male names include Bimal (pure), Rajiv (lotus, symbol of enlightenment), Deepak (light), or the name of a Hindu deity such as Krishna. Female names can be linked with God, too, such as Parvati (the consort of Shiva). Other female names include Chandra (moon), Hetal (friendly), and Asha (hope).

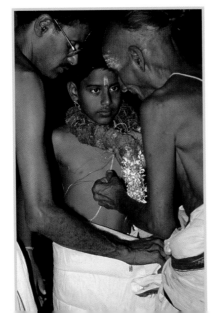

THE SACRED THREAD CEREMONY

For the first three *varnas* this ceremony marks the initiation of a boy (aged between 9 and 11) into *brahmacharya* (the student stage). The boy dresses in white to symbolize purity. He is given a sacred thread by his father or the priest, who places the thread over the boy's left shoulder. The boy promises to take his *dharma* seriously. This includes studying the scriptures.

MARRIAGE

Traditionally, Hindus believe that marriage should be based on more than just physical or emotional attraction. It is a spiritual partnership and also the joining of two families, not just two individuals. To form a strong bond, parents often arrange marriages. Today, many parents take the opinions of their children into consideration when reaching a decision.

During the marriage ceremony, the father of the bride offers his daughter's hand to the groom, asking him to cherish and love her. The groom accepts and the couple sits facing each other, separated at first by a silk curtain. They then sit side by side in front of the sacred fire (*agni*). The bride's sari is tied to the groom's clothes to symbolize their marriage.

SAPTAPADI

The most important stage of the marriage ceremony is called the *saptapadi*. This is when the bride and groom take seven steps together. Each step symbolizes the hopes that the couple has for their marriage. The steps are for food, strength, wealth, happiness, children, a long marriage, and friendship. The bride and groom also walk in a circle four, or sometimes seven, times around the fire. As they do this, the priests recite prayers from the *Vedas*.

When this stage is completed the couple is married. Family and friends invited to the wedding bless the couple. Normally, the marriage feast follows, and in the evening a reception is held.

DEATH

Funeral rites are important to most Hindus. They bring peace to the soul of the departed and provide the opportunity for relatives to grieve.

Many Hindus hope to die at home, surrounded by their family. When death is near, a drop of holy water is usually put into the dying person's mouth and family members read passages from the scriptures.

Soon after the death, funeral preparations begin. Outside India, the body may be taken straight to an undertaker, where ceremonies may be performed in a chapel. In India, the body is usually brought home. It is washed by one of the family, anointed with sandalwood paste, wrapped in a new white cloth, and laid on the floor. A small lamp is lit to guide the soul on its journey, and all family members view the body.

When a very young child or a *sannyasi* (world renouncer) dies, he or she is often buried. Otherwise, all Hindu bodies are cremated. After cremation, the family collects the ashes and scatters them, preferably in the river Ganges or another sacred river. Some Hindus outside India send the ashes to be scattered on the river Ganges. This is followed by a mourning period of about 10 to 12 days.

A FUNERAL PROCESSION
In India, a dead person's body is taken through the streets to be cremated.

15

Scriptures

The Hindu tradition has many scriptures. These can be grouped under two headings: *shruti* (revealed truths) and *smriti* (remembered truths).

READING THE SCRIPTURES
Many Hindus study the sacred scriptures to help them find spiritual guidance and also as part of their worship.

SHRUTI (REVEALED TRUTHS)

The *shruti* were revealed to holy men who interpreted them for people looking for spiritual guidance. These scriptures, regarded as timeless and everlasting, contain the *Vedas* and the *Upanishads*.

VEDAS

There are four *Vedas*, all composed between 1500 and 500 B.C. and written in the ancient language of Sanskrit. The oldest and most important is the *Rig Veda*, which is a collection of 1,028 hymns. The other three are called the *Sama, Yajur,* and *Atharva Veda*. The four *Vedas* also contain knowledge about science, mathematics, and medicine.

UPANISHADS

The *Upanishads* were written in about 800 B.C. and contain teachings about Brahman and how the soul within all living beings is also Brahman. They teach how *moksha* is achieved when the individual soul (*atman*) realizes its identity as the eternal spirit, Brahman (*see page 10*).

SMRITI (REMEMBERED TRUTHS)

The *smriti* are scriptures in the form of stories, created by holy men to help explain the teachings of the *Vedas*. The *smriti* contain the great tales of the *Ramayana* and the *Mahabharata* (written between 300 B.C.–A.D. 300), and some later scriptures called the *Puranas* (written A.D. 300 onwards). The stories in the *Puranas* tell of the religious beliefs, ideals, and values of the Hindu way of life.

MAHABHARATA

The *Mahabharata* is the longest poem in the world. It tells of a war between two families called the Kauravas (who were evil) and the Pandavas (who were good). The most famous section of the *Mahabharata* is the *Bhagavad Gita*, "The Song of the Lord." This is a description of a

conversation between the warrior prince Arjuna, who is preparing to fight a battle, and his charioteer, who is Lord Krishna. The message of the *Gita* is that devotion to God (*Bhakti yoga*) and selfless service (*Karma yoga*) are the highest forms of worship. These are the most popular forms of worship among Hindus.

RAMAYANA

The *Ramayana* is a poem which tells how Sita, Prince Rama's wife, is captured by Ravana, an evil, 10-headed demon. She is imprisoned on the island of Sri Lanka until the monkey God, Rama, rescues her with the help of Hanuman. They return to the town of Ayodhya (in northern India) where Rama becomes king. The message is that good always triumphs over evil. Many Hindus remember this story during the celebration of Diwali (*see page 24*).

Finally, the *Puranas* contain tales connected with many deities, especially Brahma, Vishnu, Shiva, and Shakti. The most popular, the *Bhagavad Purana*, tells of Vishnu and his *avatars*, including Krishna.

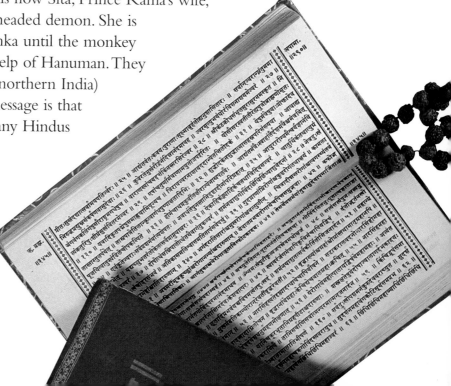

Worship and the mandir

Hindus worship both in the home and at the temple, or *mandir*. The Hindu word for worship is *puja*.

A SHRINE AT HOME
Home shrines vary greatly in size. This one in Britain is dedicated to the worship of Shiva.

OFFERINGS
Hindus make offerings to the *murti* as part of *puja*. These can include incense, food, and flowers.

WORSHIP IN THE HOME
Many Hindus worship at home in the morning and evening. Most homes have a special place, which may be a corner of a room, where *puja* is performed. The things needed to perform *puja* are kept in this area with images (*murtis*) of one or more deities, along with Hindu symbols such as the *svastika* (believed to bring good luck) or the Om symbol. There is also an incense holder and a bell.

PERFORMING PUJA
Hindus take a bath before performing *puja* so they are clean when appearing in front of God. Then a bell is rung to attract the attention of the *murti*. Incense sticks are lit to purify the air and provide a pleasant-smelling atmosphere. The person performing *puja* then says prayers and makes offerings, which may be water, milk, and foods such as fruit, rice, nuts, and sweets, to the *murti*.

The *Gayatri Mantra* is a prayer that is chanted by some Hindus at dawn, noon, and dusk. This ancient verse is the most holy of the *Vedas*. Sometimes the image of the *murti* is bathed and dressed. On other occasions a lamp is lit and the *arti* ceremony is performed (*see opposite*). During the performance of *puja* a worshiper may make a mark on his or her forehead with *kum kum* (sandalwood paste). This is known as the *tilak* mark and symbolizes the "third eye" of spiritual wisdom. The shape and color indicates the tradition to which a person belongs. A full *puja* can take over half an hour, so if a person is short of time, he or she may just light an incense stick and say a prayer. Hindus believe that even the shortest prayer is acceptable to God.

18

WORSHIP IN THE MANDIR

It is not strictly necessary for Hindus to visit a *mandir* (temple) to worship. This is because all life is believed to be sacred and everything a Hindu does may be regarded as a form of worship. In communities outside India, local people may go to the *mandir* on the weekend. As well as being places of worship, some *mandirs* are community centers and provide a place for families to meet. This gives relatives a sense of belonging and a chance to keep up with family news, especially from India.

DARSHAN

Hindus visit the *mandir* mainly to "take *darshan*." This involves viewing the *murtis* and receiving a blessing. On arriving at the *mandir*, devotees (the worshipers) remove their shoes and wash their hands. Usually, they make offerings to one or more of the *murtis* by placing flowers, milk, rice, or fruit at the shrine and saying a prayer.

PRIESTS

Each *mandir* has one or more priests, who conduct everyday services as well as special ceremonies such as weddings and funerals. Some also read people's horoscopes. Priests who devote their lives to teaching about God are often called *swami*. Priests are responsible for the upkeep and running of the temples. One of their main duties is to perform daily *puja*.

DARSHAN
Hindus make offerings to the *murti* and receive a blessing from the priest.

ARTI

Arti is a regular form of worship that takes place several times each day, especially in the morning and evening. This is a short ceremony that involves a special five-pronged lamp called an *arti* lamp. The five prongs symbolize the elements that Hindus believe make up the universe: earth, water, fire, air, and the ether (spirit). Each of the prongs holds a lighted wick. The priest waves the lamp in a clockwise direction in front of each *murti*, then brings the light down among the worshipers. They usually pass their hands over the flame and then touch their foreheads to bring the blessing of light to themselves.

CARING FOR THE MURTIS
An important part of a Hindu priest's duties includes making sure the *murtis* are well cared for.

VISHUANATH TEMPLE, NORTHERN INDIA
Temples in northern India have a tower or spire called the *shikhara*.

LOOKING AFTER THE MURTIS

Hindu temples are homes for one or more *murtis*, and an important job for the priest is to look after the *murtis* as if they were very special people, such as kings and queens. Each morning the priest awakens them with a special ritual and washes them, usually with a combination of water and milk. He then dresses the *murtis* in clothes that have often been sponsored by a Hindu family. The *murtis* are then given breakfast. Another ritual is performed at midday when the *murtis* are given lunch. After this, the curtains that surround the shrine are closed and the *murtis* are allowed to rest. At night the *murtis* are dressed in nightclothes for bed.

TEMPLE DESIGN

Hindu temples vary considerably in size and design. In particular, temples in northern India differ architecturally from temples in the south. In many European countries, temples are housed in buildings that were once used for another purpose, such as churches or even theaters. Hindus believe that the temple is a meeting place between heaven and earth.

NORTHERN INDIAN TEMPLES

In traditionally built temples in northern India, the *murtis* are placed in a central part of the building in a shrine called the *garbha-griha* (meaning "womb-house"). This is the most sacred part of the temple. Above it is a tower or spire called the *shikhara*. This symbolizes the journey of the soul towards *moksha*. Worshipers will stand before the shrine in a hall with pillars, called a *mandapa*.

SOUTHERN INDIAN TEMPLES

Southern Indian temples are significantly different from those of northern India. The building complex is usually laid out in a series of three or four concentric squares, with the main shrine housed in the innermost square. This may be a shrine to Vishnu or Shiva or the goddess Shakti. In the other squares different deities are placed around the walls. Unlike northern Indian temples, the spire above the main shrine is very short. On the outer walls of the temple there are large towers called *gopurams*. These are usually rectangular in shape and the sides taper towards the top. *Gopurams* can be up to 55 yards (50 m) in height, and they are often carved with sculptures of many different deities.

ENAKSHI TEMPLE, SOUTHERN INDIA
Temples in southern India are made up of several different buildings. This is one of the huge towers called *gopurams* that form part of the outer wall.

Sacred places

Hindus believe that many types of places, other than temples, are sacred. They include rivers and sites of important events. When a devotee makes a journey to visit one of these places, it is called a pilgrimage.

PILGRIMAGE

There are many reasons why Hindus decide to go on a pilgrimage. They might want the chance to get away from everyday life for a while, in order to concentrate fully on their religious practices and earn spiritual merit. The focus of this may be to take *darshan* (*see page 19*) and receive *prasad* (blessed food). During a pilgrimage Hindus often bathe in a holy river, visit gurus (teachers) or other holy people for spiritual advice, and see many temples or a particular famous temple. People also go on a pilgrimage in connection with one of the *samskaras* (*see pages 14–15*), or they might go in order to ask for God's help with a problem or situation in daily life, such as an illness.

PILGRIMS RESTING NEAR THE RIVER GANGES

Hindus from all around the world go on pilgrimages. They believe pilgrimages help them cross the symbolic river of life.

A place of pilgrimage is called *tirtha* in Sanskrit. It means "crossing place." Hindus believe that pilgrimages enable a person to cross the symbolic "river of life" to the shore of *moksha*. Here, he or she can be united with God and released from *samsara*, the cycle of reincarnation.

HOLY RIVERS

Rivers are important sites of pilgrimage for Hindus because they consider water to be one of the elements from which all things in the universe are created. To bathe in a holy river is thought to be like bathing in *amrit*, the original water that gave life to the world. It washes away all sins and makes all those who bathe in it holy.

THE RIVER GANGES

Most Hindus consider the river Ganges to be the holiest of all rivers. It is seen as the Mother Goddess (*Ganga Ma*) who provides for and protects all living things, especially those who come seeking her favor. Water from the river Ganges is used all over the world in worship and rituals.

22

HOLY CITIES

The cities of Varanasi and Haridwar are two of the most important pilgrimage sites in India.

VARANASI

Varanasi stands on the banks of the river Ganges in northeastern India, and is one of the oldest cities in the world. Since ancient times, it has been a great center of Hindu culture and learning. The old name for the city is Kashi, which means "resplendent with divine light."

Varanasi is a busy city dedicated to Shiva. It has an important Hindu university and many temples. The river Ganges runs through the center, where people gather on the *ghats* (steps) built on the river banks. Varanasi is famous for the cremations that take place there.

HARIDWAR

The ancient city of Haridwar, in northern India, is believed to be holy for many reasons. Most importantly, it stands at the point where the river Ganges leaves the foothills of the Himalayas and enters the plains. Haridwar is full of various types of religious people—such as *sannyasis*, gurus, priests, and astrologers—from whom pilgrims can ask advice. Priests help pilgrims perform religious ceremonies, sometimes on behalf of relatives. There are also many *ashrams* (places of spiritual retreat) where pilgrims can stay. Some *ashrams* are there specifically to help Hindus lead a holy life, to educate them, and to help them create a fair society. Because Haridwar is a holy city, meat and alcohol are not sold there.

THE KUMBHA MELA

Haridwar is one of four cities where the Kumbha Mela, one of the largest religious gatherings in the world, is held every 12 years. Kumbha Mela means "pitcher fair." In the story of the origins of the festival, the gods had been cursed and wanted to drink *amrit* (holy water) to regain their strength. The gods and demons fought over the *amrit* and the gods won the struggle. When Garuda, the giant eagle-carrier of Vishnu, took the *amrit* to heaven it spilled in four places: Nasik, Ujjain, Prayag (Allahabad), and Haridwar. These four cities host the Kumbha Mela in turn. Religious leaders, priests, gurus and their disciples, and millions of pilgrims come to the Kumbha Mela to join in the celebrations.

THE KUMBHA MELA FESTIVAL

The Kumbha Mela occurs only once every 12 years. Millions of pilgrims gather to bathe in the holy water of the rivers Ganges and Yamuna.

Festivals

Many Hindus believe all days are holy. Even the days of the week are associated with various deities. For example, Monday is Shiva's day. Religious celebrations may take place at any time, but there are also major festivals that happen just once a year.

There are a variety of Hindu festivals. Some, such as Holi, are connected with nature and the seasons of the year. Others celebrate key events in the life of a deity or a religious leader. Festivals also bring the community together to share their religious enthusiasm. Below are just a few of the most important festivals in the Hindu calendar.

DIWALI

The word *Diwali* comes from *deepawali*, which means "a row or cluster of lights." Diwali is also known as the festival of lights. It takes place in the autumn, and the five days of festivities span the end of the month of Asvina and the beginning of Karthika (sometime in October or November). There are many customs associated with Diwali, but two of them are considered the most important.

WELCOMING THE GODDESS OF WEALTH

The first custom is to invite the goddess of wealth, Lakshmi, into each home. Hindus welcome Lakshmi by lighting *divas* (little oil lamps) and making *rangoli* patterns (special designs made of colored rice paste) on the floor at the entrance to the house. It is believed that Lakshmi's visit will bring good luck and prosperity to the house in the year to come. This is important because, for many Hindus, Diwali marks the beginning of the new financial year.

CELEBRATING THE RETURN OF RAMA AND SITA

The second important aspect of Diwali is to celebrate the return of prince Rama and his wife, Sita, to their home in Ayodhya after 14 years in exile. This story is recorded in the *Ramayana* (*see pages 16–17*). Rama and Sita are highly respected, not only because Rama is seen as an *avatar* of Vishnu, but also because he demonstrated the ideal way for a person to fulfill his *dharma*.

According to the story, Rama and Sita were welcomed back home by rows of lights. In the West, many Hindus replace *divas* with colorful electric festival lights and also hold firework displays.

DIWALI

Diwali is celebrated by lighting *divas* and making *rangoli* patterns to welcome Lakshmi into each home. Many Hindus also mark the occasion with fireworks displays.

24

THE JANMASHTAMI FESTIVAL

Because Krishna was born at midnight, the street celebrations during Krishna Janmashtami, such as those shown here, go on until late in the night.

KRISHNA JANMASHTAMI

Krishna Janmashtami falls on the eighth day of the fortnight of Bhadrapada (August or September). Krishna is said to have been born at midnight on this day, more than 3,000 years before the birth of Christ. For some Hindus this is the most important festival of the year. Krishna, as an *avatar* of Vishnu, is perhaps the most popular of all Hindu deities, especially for followers of the *Bhakti yoga* of Hinduism. For them, Krishna's form and activities show most completely God's love for each and every soul. Many people fast throughout Krishna Janmashtami. Others make a partial fast, only eating fruit and drinking milk. Temples are brightly decorated. *Kirtan* (religious songs) are sung throughout the day, bells are rung, and a conch shell blown. Verses are recited from the *Bhagavad Gita* and stories are told of Krishna's birth, childhood, and later adventures. Often, at midnight, a cradle with an image of the baby Krishna is rocked and Krishna *mantras* (sacred words with special power)

are repeated. Also, in many temples offerings of butter and curds are made at midnight, in honor of Krishna's early years spent among the cowherds.

RAKSHA BANDHAN

Raksha Bandhan falls on the day of the full moon in the month of Shravana (July or August). *Raksha* means "protection" and *bandhan* means "to tie." On Raksha Bandhan, sisters tie *rakhis* (bracelets, usually made out of silk or cotton) around their brothers' wrists in order to bring them blessings and good fortune and protect them from evil. In return, brothers promise to love, protect, and care for their sisters.

Today, many Hindus send greeting cards to one another with a *rakhi* enclosed. Sometimes a woman may give a *rakhi* to a close male family friend. This symbolizes that she sees the man as an adopted brother. It is a sign of sincere friendship and a great honor. On Raksha Bandhan, men who wear the sacred thread (*see page 14*) perform a ceremony in which they remove the thread that they have worn for the past year and replace it with a new one.

Raksha Bandhan reinforces the idea of *dharma*. There are various family *dharmas*, such as the duty of parents to love their children, and the duty of children to love and respect their parents and to look after them in old age. But Raksha Bandhan focuses on the brother's *dharma*, which is to behave in a caring and affectionate way towards his sister— and the sister's *dharma* to do the same in return.

Values

The values that Hindus live by are connected with their duties (*dharma*) through the different stages of their lives. In addition, they follow a set of principles known as the *Yamas* (abstentions) and *Niyamas* (observances).

These form part of *Raj yoga*, a fourth *yoga*, the path of physical exercise and meditation.

THE FIVE YAMAS (ABSTENTIONS)

1. *Ahimsa:* do not harm any living thing (*see below*).
2. *Satya:* do not lie, be honest.
3. *Asteya:* do not steal.
4. *Brahmacharya:* do not have sexual relations outside marriage.
5. *Aparigraha:* avoid desire and greed.

THE FIVE NIYAMAS (OBSERVANCES)

1. *Shaucha:* be pure in mind, body, and speech.
2. *Santosh:* seek contentment and be satisfied with what you have.
3. *Tapa:* be prepared to make sacrifices and voluntarily accept hardship.
4. *Svadhyaya:* study the scriptures.
5. *Ishwarapranidhan:* worship daily and work with devotion.

AHIMSA

Hindu notions about the universe lead to a great respect for God, other people, and all forms of life. Because the eternal, individual soul is present in all living things, there is a strong emphasis on non-violence. This is called *ahimsa* (respect for all living things), and it can be seen as a thread running through all aspects of Hindu culture.

Ahimsa is at its strongest in Jainism, an ancient form of Hinduism founded by Mahavira, who lived about 599–527 B.C. Among Jains, *ahimsa* becomes a whole way of life. Jain monks wear a gauze mask, strain their drinks, and brush the path in front of them in order to avoid harming any living creature.

A JAIN MONK
Ahimsa is a whole way of life for Jains. They make every attempt to avoid harming living creatures, however small.

28

For many Hindus, *ahimsa* means being vegetarian and protecting the cow as a sacred animal. Some Hindus do eat meat, but vegetarian food is regarded as most pure and most appropriate for special occasions.

MOHANDAS GANDHI

Many Hindus regard Mohandas Gandhi, who was born in 1869, as a saint. Gandhi saw a lot of things wrong with Hindu society, especially the way people treated the untouchables. He called the untouchables "Harijans," which means "children of God." He persuaded many Hindus that untouchables should be allowed to enter temples and to live their lives like any other group in society.

Gandhi believed in protesting without violence. This was his way of interpreting the idea of *ahimsa* to make it relevant to all aspects of life. During his life, Gandhi went on 17 fasts as political acts. In 1932, he fasted, saying he was willing to die, in protest against the way Indian society treated the untouchables. He also fasted to prevent violence.

In 1947, Gandhi was a key person in leading India into independence from the British, who had ruled there since 1763. Not everyone agreed with Gandhi, and because of this he was assassinated in 1948. However, his followers gave him the title of "Mahatma," which means "great soul."

MAHATMA GANDHI ADDRESSING A CROWD AT BEZWADA ASSAM, 1946
Gandhi believed in protesting without using violence. Instead, he often fasted to achieve his goals.

29

Key questions and answers

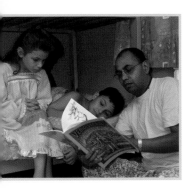

WHAT IS HINDUISM? Hinduism is one of the oldest religions in the world. It has been around for at least 5,000 years. It is the main religion of India. For Hindus, it is much more than a religion; it is a way of life based on understanding natural and everlasting principles (*see pages 4–5*).

HOW MANY HINDUS ARE THERE WORLDWIDE? Approximately 807 million.

WHAT ARE THE PATHS OF HINDUISM? The spiritual paths of Hinduism are called *yogas*. The main *yogas* are: *Bhakti, Jnana, Karma,* and *Raj.*

WHAT DO HINDUS BELIEVE? Hinduism stresses the idea of *dharma*, the performance of duties according to an individual's nature. The central goal of most Hindus is to achieve *moksha*. They believe that the soul lives many times before becoming pure enough to reach *moksha* (*see pages 10–13*). Many Hindus believe there is one God who is worshiped in different forms (*see pages 6–9*).

WHAT ARE THE HINDU SCRIPTURES CALLED? The Hindu tradition has many scriptures. These are grouped under two headings: *shruti*, or revealed truths, and *smriti*, or remembered truths (*see pages 16–17*).

WHAT DOES HINDUISM TEACH PEOPLE ABOUT LIFE? For Hindus, life is a journey from one body to another, and this one life is in itself a journey from birth to death (*see page 10*). Life is divided into four stages, called *ashramas*. The *ashramas* are: *brahmacharya, grihasta, vanaprastha,* and *sannyasa* (*see pages 12–13*). Most Hindus follow a set of principles known as the *Yamas* and *Niyamas* (*see pages 28–29*).

WHERE DO HINDUS WORSHIP? Hindus worship in a special place at home and in temples called *mandirs* (*see pages 18–21*). Hindus also believe many places are sacred (*see pages 22–23*).

WHAT ARE THE MAIN HINDU FESTIVALS?

Diwali, Krishna Janmashtami, Raksha Bandhan, and *Holi* (*see pages 24–27*). Many Hindus believe all days are holy.

Glossary

AGNI A sacred fire.

AHIMSA Reverence for all living things. A key Hindu value, practiced especially by Jains.

AMRIT Holy water—the original water, that gave life to the world.

ARTHA Earning one's living by honest means. One of the four aims of life for Hindus.

ARTI A ceremony in which light is offered to the deities and then to the devotees.

ASHRAMAS The four stages of a Hindu's life. Each stage has its own *dharma*.

ATMAN The eternal, individual self. The soul, or divine spark of Brahman within all living beings.

AVATAR One who descends. A*vatars* of Vishnu include Rama and Krishna.

AVIDYA Ignorance of spiritual truth.

AYODHYA A town in northern India believed to be the birthplace of Rama; a place of pilgrimage.

DARSHAN A glimpse of a deity.

DHARMA The performance of duties according to an individual's nature. For example, the *dharma* of fire is to be hot, the *dharma* of sugar is to be sweet.

GANGA MA Literally, "the Mother Goddess;" the name given to the holy river Ganges.

HOLI Spring festival of colors.

JAINISM An Indian religious movement whose key figure was Mahavira (599–527 B.C.), and that emphasizes *ahimsa* as a key value.

KAMA Enjoying life's pleasures. One of the four goals in life for Hindus.

KARMA The law of cause and effect.

KUMBHA MELA The largest and most important Hindu pilgrimage festival, held every 12 years.

LINGUM One of the representations of Shiva.

MAHABHARATA The longest poem in the world.

MANDIR A Hindu temple.

MANTRA A short, sacred text or prayer that is said repeatedly and helps to focus the mind.

MAYA Illusion—having the wrong ideas about what really matters and what is really true.

MOKSHA Liberation from the wheel of *samsara*.

MURTI Literally "form." The image of a deity used in worship.

OM A sacred symbol representing the original sound made when the Supreme created the universe.

PRAKRITI Refers to the matter from which the temporary body is made.

PUJA Worship.

RAMAYANA A Hindu epic that relates the story of Rama and Sita.

SAMSARA The tiring wheel of suffering and misery. The cycle of birth, death, and reincarnation.

SANATANA DHARMA The eternal way. Most Hindus prefer this name for their religion.

SANNYASI A person at the fourth stage of life, a "world renouncer."

SHAKTI Feminine divine energy or power.

TIRTHA A place of pilgrimage.

TRIMURTI A three-form representation of the life force of Brahman.

UPANISHADS Sacred texts that explain the meaning of the *Vedas*.

VARNAS The four class divisions in Hindu society.

VEDAS *Veda* means knowledge. Hindus believe that the four *Vedas* are revealed truths or *shruti*.

YOGA A spiritual path.

YOGI Someone who meditates following *Jnana yoga*.

Index

agni (sacred fire) 15, 31
ahimsa (respect for all living things) 28–29, 31
amrit (holy water) 22, 23, 31
artha (earning an honest living) 12, 31
arti ceremony 18, 19, 31
Aryan migration 4
ashramas 12, 13, 30, 31
  brahmacharya 12, 14, 30
  grihasta 12, 30
  sannyasa 13, 15, 23, 30
  vanaprastha 13, 30
ashrams (places of spiritual retreat) 23
atman (individual soul) 5, 6, 10, 16, 31
avatar 8, 9, 31
  of Vishnu 9, 24, 26
avidya (ignorance of spiritual truth) 7, 10, 31
Ayodhya 17

Brahma 6, 8, 17
brahman (God) 4
Brahman (the Supreme) 4, 5, 6, 7, 10, 16

caste *see jatis and varnas*
cremation 10, 15, 23

darshan 19, 22, 31
death 5, 10, 14, 15
deities 6, 8, 18, 21
dharma 4, 12, 13, 14, 24, 27, 28, 30, 31
divas (little oil lamps) 24
Diwali 17, 24
Durga 8

fasting 27, 29
festivals 24–27, 30

Gandhi, Mahatma 5, 29
Ganges, river 4, 9, 15, 22, 23
ghats (steps) 23
gurus 12, 22, 23

Haridwar 23
Himalayas 7, 23
Hindu population 4, 30

ignorance 7, 8, 10

India 4, 5, 9, 13, 15, 17, 19, 23, 29
Indus valley 4

Jainism 28, 31
jatis 5
journey of life 10–13, 14

Kali 8
kama 12, 31
karma 10, 31
Krishna 5, 8, 9, 14, 17, 26, 27
Kumbha Mela, the 23, 31

Lakshmi 8, 24
lotus flower 7

Mahabharata see scriptures
Mahishasura (buffalo demon) 8
marriage 14, 15
  saptapadi 15
maya (illusion) 10, 31
meditation 5, 6, 7, 13, 28
moksha (spiritual freedom) 5, 7, 10, 12, 13, 20, 22, 30, 31
Mother Nature 8
murti (form) 6, 9, 18, 19, 20, 31

Niyamas (observances) 28, 30

Om 6, 18, 31

Parvati 8, 14
pilgrimage 22, 23
prakriti 6, 31
prasad (blessed food) 22
prayer 14, 15, 18, 19
  Gayatri Mantra 18
priests 14, 19, 20, 23
  swami 19

rakhis (bracelets) 27
Rama 8, 9, 17, 24
Ramanuja 4, 5
Ramayana see scriptures
reincarnation 5, 10, 22
rituals 14, 20, 22

sacred thread, the 12, 14, 27
samsara (eternal cycle of death and reincarnation) 5, 10, 22, 31
samskaras 14–15, 22

Sanatana Dharma (the eternal religion) 4, 31
Sanskrit 16, 17, 22
Saraswati 8
scriptures 4, 12, 15, 16–17, 28
  shruti (revealed truths) 16, 30
    Upanishads, the 16, 31
    Vedas, the 4, 9, 12, 15, 16, 17, 18, 31
  smriti (remembered truths) 16, 17, 30
    Mahabharata 9, 16, 31
    Puranas 16, 17
    Ramayana 9, 16, 17, 24, 31
Shaivas 8
Shakti 8, 17, 21, 31
Shankara 4, 5, 10
Shiva 6, 7, 8, 14, 17, 21, 23, 24
  lingum 7
shrines 18, 19, 20, 21
  garbha-griha 20
souls 5, 6, 10, 15, 16, 28

temples (*mandirs*) 6, 7, 18, 19, 20–21, 22, 23, 27, 29, 30, 31
tilak mark, the 18
tirtha (a place of pilgrimage) 22, 31
Trimurti, the 6, 31

Uma 8
untouchables 5, 29

Vaishnavas 8
Varanasi 23
varnas (classes) 5, 9, 12, 14, 31
  Brahmins 5
  Kshatriyas 5
  Shudras 5
  Vaishyas 5
Vedanta 4
Vedas, the *see scriptures*
Vishnu 6, 7, 8, 17, 21, 23, 24

worship (*puja*) 5, 6, 16, 17, 18–19, 22, 28, 31

Yamas (abstentions) 28, 30
yogas 4, 5, 9, 30, 31
  Bhakti yoga 5, 17, 26, 30
  Jnana yoga 5, 30
  Karma yoga 5, 17, 30
  Raj yoga 28, 30
yogi 5, 7, 31